Children of Another Planet

I Talk You Talk Press

CONTENTS

1. THE STRANGE DRAWING

My name is Ai Hayashi. I'm 17. I go to high school. In my class there are 20 boys and 17 girls. I know all the girls, but I don't have a special friend.

Friends belong to the same sports club, or go to the department stores after school, or study in the library together. I don't do those things, so that's why I don't have a special friend.

Girls in my class don't talk to the boys. The boys don't talk to the girls. There's a girls' circle and a boys' circle. That's the way it is.

I'm not pretty, but I think I look OK. Except for my nose. My nose is different. I say my father is American. I say 'he is American' but maybe he 'was American'. I don't know if he is alive or dead. I don't know his name. Maybe my mother knows, but she doesn't want to talk about him. I don't ask her questions anymore. She never answers. He went away before I was born, so, I pretend he was an American.

When I started at this school I was teased about my nose. People said, "Eagle nose!"

I lied. I said that my father came from the north of Japan. I said he was a businessman. I said noses like mine are common in the north. I said I had my father's nose.

Every day, when classes finish, I go home. Sometimes other girls ask me to go shopping with them, or to Starbucks for a coffee. I always say, "Thank you, but not today. I have something to do."

I walk home. I bring in the laundry. I cook something for my mother and me to eat. I do my homework. Most days I can finish everything by 7:00pm. I eat dinner with my mother when she comes home from work at about 9:30pm. Until then, I have two and a half wonderful hours to myself. I read, or I play my cello. My mother doesn't like to hear me play my cello. Maybe it's because I play so badly. So I only play it when I'm alone in the apartment.

Sometimes I have something else very special to do. I will tell you about that later. I don't need a special friend. I have no time. My life is full, and I am happy.

This semester we have a new teacher. He likes students to change desks every week. This week I am sitting at the back of the classroom. I am sitting next to Mori-kun. He is very tall. His hair is a little curly. He only came to the school this year. Everyone likes him, but he has no special friend. As soon as classes finish, he leaves school very quickly on his bicycle.

It is a math class. Mori-kun is not listening to the teacher. He is looking at a piece of paper. I put my textbook up in front of my face so that no one can see me, and I look at him. He seems very tired. His face is pale.

Mr Kimura likes to ask students to write their homework answers on the blackboard. I have my homework in front of me. Mori-kun only has the piece of paper on his desk.

"Mori-kun," says Mr Kimura. "Please come and show the class how to solve question number three."

Mori-kun doesn't hear him. He seems to be asleep. I hit him on the arm. He blinks and shakes his head.

"Mori-kun!" Mr Kimura is getting angry. I give Mori-kun my homework.

"Go on! Quickly!" I say. "Write the answer to question three on the blackboard."

He takes my book and goes to the front of the room. He looks like a sleepwalker. While he is gone, I look at the piece of paper. I get a shock. Mori-kun has drawn eight black dots. The dots make a circle but the circle is not finished. It needs two more dots to make a perfect circle. It doesn't look like anything special, but I have seen it before!

2. FLYING

I said that sometimes I have something very special to do after school. This is true. My mother and I live in an old apartment. It has two balconies. One is outside the kitchen and living room. We hang the laundry out there. The other balcony is outside my mother's room. It is very narrow. There is a wall at the edge of the balcony and then a tall iron fence above it. She never goes out there. There is an old chair. It looks like one of those chairs with long footrests that you sometimes see in movies or TV shows. They are next to swimming pools, and beautiful people are sitting on them.

The wall of the apartment is next to this chair on one side, and the balcony fence on the other. I am the only person who sits in this chair.

Let me tell you what happens.

It starts a few years ago. I'm still in junior high school. It's summer vacation. My mother is at work, so I'm home alone. It's very hot. It's so hot in the apartment, I can't breathe. I decide to take my book and sit on the chair on the balcony. It's dirty, so I take some old cushions and a towel.

I think, *I can imagine I am a beautiful person by a swimming pool at a luxury hotel.*

I sit on the chair. I start reading, but something very strange happens. I'm flying through clouds. My clothes are different. I'm wearing a blue body suit, with long sleeves and legs that come down past my knees. I'm travelling very quickly, and I'm looking for something.

Then, suddenly, I'm back in my normal clothes. I'm sitting on the chair and holding my book. I fell asleep, I think. *What a crazy dream!*

I often sit on the chair on the balcony during the summer. Sometimes nothing happens, but sometimes I have the flying dream. It's always the same. I'm wearing tight blue clothes, and I'm looking for something.

I start to worry. It's not normal to have the same dream many times. I never have the dream when I'm in bed, only when I'm sitting on the balcony chair.

I stop sitting out on the balcony. When summer vacation ends, I go back to school, and I forget about the strange dreams.

A few months later, I'm playing my cello when I get a strange feeling. It's like a voice in my head. The voice tells me to go out onto the balcony. It's cold, so I put on my coat and take a blanket. I hurry. It seems to be urgent. I sit down on the chair and suddenly I'm flying. My tight blue clothes are the same, but the clouds are different. They are dark and cold. Once again, I'm looking for something. Then I see a stone falling through the clouds. I dive through the clouds and catch it.

I come back to my chair. I'm wearing my coat, the blanket is still on the chair, but I'm holding a stone!

The flying events aren't dreams! They're real!

I look at the stone. It's the size of a watermelon. It's shiny black with blue spots in it. It feels warm.

I'm very frightened. What is happening to me? I put the stone under the chair and go back inside.

I run to the mirror in my mother's bedroom and look at myself. I look the same as usual. I don't tell anyone about this. Who could I tell?

3. AI IS FRIGHTENED

Over the next two years, the same thing happens nine more times. It's always the same. A voice in my head tells me I have to go to the balcony. I try to ignore it, but I always go. Sometimes the clouds are white and fluffy; sometimes they are grey or black. But a stone falls through the clouds and I catch it. On my seventeenth birthday I collect the last stone. There are now ten stones under the chair.

How do I know it's the last stone? I know, because this year it changes.

I've been flying three times this year. But now, I'm not looking for stones, I'm delivering them.

The first time, it happens like this.

I get the feeling that tells me I must go to the balcony. The voice tells me to take two stones from under the chair. Then I'm flying, but I'm carrying two stones. They feel heavy and I don't fly as well as usual.

The clouds are white. They open up and for the first time I see the ground far below me. I'm not frightened. I can see a green field. On one side of the field there is a flat area with a circle of stones around the edge. They are the same size as the stones I am carrying, but they are grey. In the middle of the circle is another, larger stone.

On the other side of the field I can see another flat area. I fly down and put the stones down on the ground.

Then I'm back in the chair on the balcony.

I do the same thing three times. There are only four stones left under the chair.

The day before I see Mori-kun's drawing, I go flying again. But this time is a little different. When I fly down with the two stones, I feel frightened. I'm not scared of flying. There is something down in the field that is dangerous. I don't want to go there, but I do.

I add the stones to the circle, but I can't go back to the apartment balcony. The air feels heavy. I have a very bad feeling. I panic. Then something happens. For the first time, I see something like a person. It's a shape, but it is carrying a long stick. The stick flashes, and I'm back on the balcony.

I sit in the chair. I'm shaking. I don't like this! I'm never going back! I must be strong. When the voice in my head tells me to go to the balcony, I won't go!

4. MORI-KUN TALKS TO AI

Mori-kun comes back to his desk. He puts my homework notebook on my desk. Mr Kimura is asking another student to write a homework question on the board. Mori-kun takes his math book out of his bag. He seems normal. He doesn't look at me.

All day, I wonder about Mori-kun, and the drawing. I leave school and walk home. I get a surprise. Mori-kun is waiting on the street. He has his bicycle. I walk up to him. He smiles. "Thank you for helping me out in school today," he says.

"That's OK," I say. "Sometimes Mr Kimura is very tough. I didn't want him to shout at you."

"Thank you," he says again. He gets on his bicycle to ride away.

"Hey!" I shout. "Can I ask you something?"

He stops and looks at me.

"The drawing on your desk. What was it?" I ask.

"Nothing special," he says. "Why?"

I look at the ground. I look at the sky. I don't know what to say.

"Why?" he asks again.

"Because it looked like the stone circles!"

He jumps forward. His bike falls on the ground, but he doesn't notice. "What about the stones?" he whispers. His face is very close to mine. His face has gone white.

I'm frightened. "Oh, nothing. Forget I said anything."

"What about the stones?" he whispers again.

I say something crazy. I say, "I have two more stones to deliver, but it's getting more difficult."

He looks at me. He shakes his head. "Unbelievable!" Then he smiles. "Do you live near here?"

I point to the building behind us. "I live there."

"Can I come inside with you?"

I don't know what to do. My mother will be very angry if I invite a boy to our apartment when she is not home. But then I think, *He's not my boyfriend. I'll be OK. He's not interested in me. He knows something about the stones. I want to know what they mean. I want to know why I fly. I want to know what happened in the field.*

So I say, "OK."

He picks up his bike. We walk over to the apartment building. I show him where he can put his bike. We ride up in the elevator together. I feel strange and nervous. I have never had a boyfriend. I have never asked a friend from school to come to the apartment.

Inside the apartment I say, "Please sit down. Would you like something to drink?" I sound like a waitress in a restaurant, but I don't know what to say.

Our living room is very small. We never have visitors, so there are only two armchairs. He is sitting in my mother's chair. I pour some tea into a glass and give it to him.

"Thank you," he says. He looks different. Down on the street he frightened me, but now he seems relaxed. I think he looks happy.

I sit down in my armchair.

"Tell me about the stones," I say.

He doesn't answer. He looks around the room. He sees my cello. "You play the cello," he says.

"Yes."

He looks at my cello. "It's a very good cello," he says. "Where did you get it from?"

I feel stupid. "I don't know," I answer. "I've always had it."

"Do you belong to the school orchestra?" he asks.

"No. I just play it here at home."

"Do you have a music teacher?"

"No. I just play it. I play very badly, but I like to play."

He comes back and sits down in my mother's chair. He picks up the glass of tea. He looks at me. "I play the violin," he says. "I never had a lesson, but I play. I don't know why or how."

Then he doesn't say anything. He sits and drinks tea. I feel angry. "I think you should go now," I say.

"The stones," he says slowly. "The first time I saw the stones was yesterday. It was the first time I went to that place. I saw someone. I guess it was you. I don't know who you are. But I don't know who I am either. Sometimes I'm not here. Sometimes I'm somewhere else."

I'm excited. He will understand! "You fly too!" I say. "Isn't it strange?"

He looks surprised. "I don't fly!"

"Oh." My face is red. He will think I am crazy. I just told him I could fly!

He looks at me. His face is red too. "I don't fly. I carry a sword. I don't know why, but sometimes I have to do something."

We talk and talk. I tell Mori-kun everything that has happened. He tells me what has happened to him.

5. MORI-KUN'S STORY

Mori-kun started going to other places when he was younger than me. "The first time, I was about ten years old. I was running home from school," he says.

"I'm always moving when it happens. I'm running or walking, or I'm climbing stairs. Then I'm in another place. Sometimes someone is chasing me. Other times I'm just running, like I'm going somewhere. My clothes are different."

"Do you wear a kind of racing swimsuit?"

"No. I have shorts and a T-shirt. They are made out of some shiny blue material. And I have boots. They are made from the same material but it is much thicker. I'm always wearing the same clothes."

"My clothes are blue too."

"When I was young, I was always running in a forest. Now I'm older, I'm often in a field."

"The field where the stones are?"

"No. Somewhere else. First I have a long stick. I swing it. I seem to be practicing. I practice jumping and running too. I get very tired. Then two years ago, the stick changed to a sword."

"I think you were very frightened when you were only ten years old and you couldn't tell anyone about it," I say.

"But, I did tell someone. I was living with my grandfather. I told him."

"What did he say?"

"He said, 'Your mother'. But he didn't say anything else. But we moved to another city. Every two or three months, it happened again. I told him every time. We moved around the south of Japan, but it didn't make any difference. Then we went to Hokkaido, in the countryside. We stayed there for a long time. He never said anything, but I knew he worried about it."

I shiver. I feel cold. The room is getting darker. I look at my mobile phone. We have been talking for hours! I want to hear about the drawing. I have so many questions. But I say, "My mother will be home soon. You must go. I must cook food for her."

He gets up. "We can't talk at school," he says. "No one must know. I will come to see you here. Can I have your phone number?"

I give him my number and he gives me his.

We walk to the door. He turns and looks at me. "It's nice not to feel so alone." Then he goes away.

6. THE BIG OLD HOUSE

The next day Mori-kun is not at school. I feel very bad. Maybe he is sorry he talked to me?

At lunchtime I get a text message on my phone. It's an address. I know it is from Mori- kun.

I send a text back ---*'Shall I come and see you?'*---

I get a one-word answer. ---*'Yes'*---.

After school I go home and bring in the laundry. I cook some food for my mother and me to eat later. I look at the maps on the Internet and find out how to get to the address. It is only 5:30pm. If I walk quickly, I can get there in about 20 minutes.

I hurry out of the apartment and take the elevator down to the street. I find the house. It is very big and old. There is a big heavy gate. It is closed. Suddenly, I'm nervous. I don't know what I will find inside. I stand in the street and look up at the house. On the second floor there is an open window. Someone is waving to me. I push the gate open and walk through the garden to the main door. It is closed but I open it and go inside. Mori-kun's bicycle is in the porch. The house is very quiet. It seems empty. It doesn't look like anyone lives there. There is a little furniture, but the only shoes in the porch are a pair of sports shoes. I guess they are Mori-kun's.

"Hello!" I say

"Hayashi-san! Upstairs!" I hear Mori-kun's voice.

I don't feel happy. I'm a little scared. The house is old and dark. I don't like it.

"Hayashi-san!" I hear Mori-kun's voice again.

I take off my shoes and go into the house. I walk up the stairs. I see a long hallway with three doors. One of the doors is open. I walk to the door and look in.

Mori-kun is lying on a bed near the window.

"Thanks for coming," he says.

"Oh, no!" I shout. "What happened?"

One side of Mori-kun's face is very red and swollen. One eye is closed. He looks terrible, but he smiles.

"You can see why I didn't go to school today."

"What happened?" I ask again.

"I'll tell you everything. But could you get me something to drink please? I hurt my leg too."

I look around the room. It's big. There is a large table. On one end of the table are schoolbooks and a computer. The other end is next to a small kitchen. Mori-kun has a rice cooker, a toaster oven, a gas ring and a small refrigerator. Next to the table are some shelves with pots and a kettle, and food.

"What do you want? Shall I make some tea or coffee?"

"There's a can of orange juice in the refrigerator. Could I have that please? And then some coffee would be great. Thank you."

I give Mori-kun the juice.

"You have to go down to the main kitchen for water," he says.

I take the kettle and go downstairs. I think it's very strange, but I don't feel frightened anymore. I fill the kettle in the kitchen downstairs. It's empty. I can see that no one uses it. I carry the kettle upstairs. I make coffee. I take a chair and put it next to the bed. Mori-kun looks better. I give him a cup of coffee.

"Tell me everything!" I say.

7. OUR NAMES ARE THE SAME

"After I left your apartment last night, I was very excited. It's amazing to meet someone who has a life like mine. I biked home very fast. I was running upstairs to this room when the usual thing happened. I was in the other world.

"I was running towards the circle of stones – the one that you are making. I had my sword. It was the same as the last time. The time when I saw you.

"It was almost dark. I knew there was danger. I looked up and there was a very big bird. It was black. It was in the sky above my head. It came down, closer and closer. I thought it wanted to attack me, but it picked up one of the stones. I ran towards it and I jumped up as high as I could and used my sword. A light like a laser beam came out of the sword. I know I hit it because it made a terrible noise, dropped the stone and flew away. But one of its wings hit my face and knocked me over.

"I woke up on the stairs. My leg was hurting a lot. I got into bed and fell asleep. When I woke up, I sent you the text message. Thank you for coming."

"That's OK. I wanted to see you. I wanted to talk," I say. "Are you hungry? I'll cook something for you."

"I'm starving." Mori-kun smiles again. He looks strange because only half his face smiles. The other half is so red and swollen it doesn't move.

I find some food in the refrigerator. I start to make noodles and fried vegetables with tofu. I'm a good cook.

Mori-kun lies on the bed and watches me. He doesn't speak. It makes me feel nervous.

"Why are you so quiet?" I ask.

"I'm thinking. We have to understand what is happening. It's dangerous now. You might get hurt. Maybe we have to find a way to stop going to this other place before one of us is killed."

"Why are we the same?" I ask.

"I was thinking about that. What's your first name?"

"Ai," I say.

"Ai. I like it. Can I call you Ai?"

My face goes red. "OK. If you want to."

"There are a lot of ways to write the character for Ai," he says. "How do you write your name?"

"Like the colour, 'indigo'." I wonder what Mori-kun is thinking.

He takes a pencil and a notebook from the small table next to the bed.

He writes something. "Look at this."

I stop chopping vegetables, and go to look at the paper.

"This is my name," he says. He points to the Chinese characters. "And this is your name."

I look at the four characters he has written.

"Our names are the same," he says quietly. "Our family name is forest and our first name is blue. You are Ai and I am Sei. Please call me Sei."

"OK." I don't understand.

Then he asks. "Are you my sister?"

I feel angry. I like Sei. But I don't want him to be my brother.

"Of course not!" I say loudly. "That's a crazy idea." I go back to the table. The water for the noodles is boiling.

Sei is quiet again. I make the meal. I don't look at him. When I take the bowl of noodles and vegetables and tofu to the bed I see that his face looks very sad. I feel sorry for him.

"Please eat," I say. "I'm sorry I shouted. Your idea was such a surprise."

Sei takes the bowl and the chopsticks. "Thank you. I'm sorry too. But I guess I'm lonely. There was only my grandfather and me. Now there is only me. I would love to have a sister."

"Where is your grandfather now?" I ask.

"We were in Hokkaido, and he got sick. He said we should move here. We came in February. He was dying. He told me he was a priest. He said that he left the temple to look after me. But he wanted to go back to his temple on Mount Myoken to die. We went there, and he died very soon after. The people at the temple did everything. Then I came back here. My grandfather told me to live a normal life. He said I must not tell anyone that he was dead. He fixed everything with the bank. So I always have money. The house is too big for me. But I can't move because I'm too young to rent an apartment. Someone would find out that I live alone. So I made this room for myself and this is where I live."

"What about your parents? Do you have any other family?"

"I don't think so. My grandfather said my parents died when I was very small. But when he was dying, he told me that my mother left as soon as I was born. My father went to look for her, but he never came back. What about you?"

"My mother told me my father was not Japanese. I think maybe he was American. I think I have an American nose. I don't know his name. She won't tell me anything else. She says we have no family. I don't know where I was born. I love my mother, but she won't talk about the past."

Sei eats some more noodles. "These are very good. I guess we are not related."

"Why?"

"Because I can't cook!"

I look at my phone. It's 8:30pm! I have to go.

"Sei. I'm sorry. I have to go soon. My mother will come home. But I don't want to leave you. Can we call a taxi, and you can go to the hospital?"

"No, I can't do that. I'm underage. They will want to contact my family."

"What shall we do? I can't leave you here alone."

"Yes you can. I'll be OK. I'm tired again. I'll sleep. In the morning I'll feel better."

I take the noodle bowl. I bring a jug of water and put it next to the bed. I put rice in the rice cooker and set the timer for the next morning.

Then I go. I run all the way back to my house. When my mother arrives home, I'm sitting doing my homework.

"Did you have a lot of homework?" she asks.

"Yes, a lot," I answer. I get up and put the meal on the table. We eat. I wash the dishes and then we watch television together. It seems like any other night.

8. YOU MUST TALK TO YOUR MOTHER

My mother leaves for work at 7:00am. As soon as she leaves the house, I call the school. I say I am my mother. "Ai has a terrible toothache," I say. "She will have to go to the dentist today. She won't come to school. Please tell her homeroom teacher."

I go to Sei's house. The main door is unlocked. I run up the stairs. He is not in his room! "Sei! Sei! Where are you?" I shout. I can hear Sei's voice. He is downstairs.

I run down the stairs. "Where are you?"

"In the bathroom. I want to take a shower. Just wait. I'll be with you soon."

I go back to Sei's room. I tidy up and start making breakfast.

When I hear Sei on the stairs, I go out to help him. He is moving very slowly, but he can walk. He looks worse because his face is turning black, but he says he feels much better.

We sit together at the table and eat breakfast.

"You should be at school," he says.

"I know. But I can't go to school and leave you alone here."

"Why not? I'm always alone. It's OK."

"Maybe it's OK when you are well. But you still have pain. And we have to decide what to do."

"I've been thinking," says Sei. "We don't know why this is happening. We don't know what the connection is between us. We don't have any answers. All we know that is you and I have a job to do."

"Yes. My job is to collect the stones and take them to the field.

But what's your job?" I ask.

Sei looks strange. "I don't know. Maybe it sounds crazy. But all that practice - the running and jumping, and the sword. I think my job is to be a warrior."

"To fight a war?" I ask.

"No. Maybe my job is to protect the stone circles. Or maybe to protect you?"

"Who is the enemy?" I ask.

"The bird is an enemy," says Sei.

"What are the circles?" I ask Sei. "What do they mean?" But Sei doesn't know.

"You have to deliver two more stones," he says.

"Then it will be finished," I say. I'm frightened. I don't want to do this anymore.

"No," says Sei. "Think about the other circle. It has the big stone too."

"Maybe I could fly with a stone like that, but I couldn't catch it," I say. "I think it would be too heavy. Will you be there the next time I'm called to deliver the stones?"

Sei shakes his head. "I don't know. It makes me angry. Someone or something is controlling us. I wish we knew more."

I take the dishes from the table. "I'm going down to the kitchen to wash these."

I go downstairs. The house is so quiet. It makes me nervous. When I come back, Sei has gone.

I know he has gone to the other place. I'm worried. His leg is very bad and so is his face. How can he do anything? If the bird attacks him, he won't be able to run or jump.

And something is different. Sei told me he always goes to the other place when he is running or moving. This time he was sitting still.

I sit in Sei's room for hours. His violin is on a chair in the corner of the room. I pick it up and try to play it. I can't. I can play the cello, but the violin is different. I look at all his books. He likes the same kind of books as I do. I switch on his computer and watch videos on YouTube. Time passes slowly. I make coffee. I eat some bread.

Suddenly he is back! I don't hear anything or see anything, but he is sitting in the chair at the table.

He is very cold. He is shivering. I find a sweatshirt on the floor and give it to him. I pour a cup of coffee for him.

"Ai! Someone spoke to me! I was on a mountain. It was snowing. I was sitting on a stone bench. My face hurt and my leg hurt. I was cold. I didn't have my sword. Then I started walking through the snow. It was very difficult. I was very slow, but I knew I must keep moving. I came to the edge of the cliff – for the first time I could see everything."

"What do you mean? Everything?" I'm puzzled. I don't understand.

Sei drinks some more coffee. "I told you. In the beginning I was always running in a forest. Then later, I was in a field practicing to be a warrior. Then there was the field with the stone circles."

"Yes. They are different places."

"From the mountain I looked down into an open space. There are mountains all around. They make a circle. It was like looking down into a round dish. Inside the circle there is a forest, some flat green areas and a big stone building. It looks like a castle. In the centre of the circle is a round space. I was too high up to see, but I think that is where the stone circles are. It has trees around it.

"Then I thought there was someone sitting next to me. I couldn't see anyone, but I could feel someone. There was a voice. Someone was talking. It was a man. I don't know if it was a voice in my head, or if someone invisible was sitting next to me."

"What did he say?"

Sei is quiet. "I don't want you to think I am crazy. It was something like this… 'You have done well, but you must do better. We have many children on Earth, but only a few have our powers. Only four of our children are time and space travellers. We don't know why this is so. But so it is. So you, and Ai Hayashi, and her half-brother in America, and the little one in France, are our only hope.'

Sei looks at me and I look at him. "We are time and space travellers," he says.

I feel angry. "We know that," I say. "We know we travel in time and space. But what does 'our children' mean?"

"And did you know you have a half-brother in America?" asks Sei.

"No! Of course not! And what about the 'little one' in France? We don't know anything!"

"No. We don't," says Sei. "But we are part of a plan. I want to know what the plan is. I wish I had asked my grandfather more questions. Ai, you must talk to your mother. I'm sorry, but you must be strong. Please try to talk to her."

9. AI'S MOTHER'S STORY

I help Sei to lie down on his bed. I make some food and put it next to the bed. I give him a glass of water, and I leave.

I go back to the apartment. I make food for a meal. It is 6:30pm. My mother will come home about 9:30pm. I have no homework, because I didn't go to school. I don't know what to do. I want to play my cello. I also want to sit on the chair outside my mother's window. But there is no space for the cello on the balcony.

I walk up and down our small apartment. Then I open the door to the balcony outside my mother's room. I sit on her bed and I play my cello.

When I play my cello, I'm in another world. The music takes me to another place. I hear a voice. The voice says, "Ai, you are our daughter. You and Sei are the strongest of our children. We need you."

"I don't understand," I say.

"I will tell you and Sei the story soon. Be ready. The time will come very soon. Your half-brother will help you. You must save our people."

"But!" I shout.

I hear my mother come into the apartment.

I hurry to put food on the table. My mother comes and sits with me. She looks very tired.

"Your homeroom teacher called me at work. He asked about your toothache. What did you do today?"

I don't say anything. I'm very worried. I can't tell my mother about Sei. I can't tell my mother about the flying, or the voice in my head.

"Are you unhappy at school?" my mother asks.

"No. I like school. But I don't understand my life. It's very difficult. I'm different from other students in my class. I know it's because of my father. Please tell me about him."

My mother eats some food. She looks very unhappy. I feel very bad.

"It's OK," I say. "You don't have to tell me."

"Please make some tea for me," says my mother.

I make the tea, and my mother and I sit facing each other.

"I met your father just after I finished university," she says. "I had no family, and I was lonely. He was a wonderful man - so tall and strong and handsome. I fell in love with him the first time I saw him. He looked like a star athlete, but he was a musician.

"He played in an orchestra. The other people in the orchestra talked about him. They said he didn't need to read music. He could hear a sonata, or a symphony just one time and he could play it perfectly. He said the music came out of his head.

"I thought he loved me as much as I loved him. But I was wrong. For just one year I thought we were very happy. Then you were born. He named you Ai. Then he came to me one day, and said he must leave. He seemed sad, but he wouldn't tell me why he was going. He left that cello for you, and he disappeared.

"I thought I would go crazy. I looked for him. I paid private detectives to find out where he had gone. All they could tell me was that he had taken a plane to the USA. I couldn't do anything more. I had no more money and I had you. You were only a few weeks old."

"So he went back home to America?" I ask.

My mother shakes her head. "I told you he was American, but I don't know. It was strange. He spoke Japanese perfectly, but he spoke English perfectly too. He never said anything about his family, or his past and I didn't ask. I was so much in love, and so happy."

I jump up and put my arms around my mother. "I'm so sorry. It must have been hard for you."

"Maybe I should have told you. But it hurt me too much to think about it or talk about it."

"It's OK," I say. "I understand. I'm sorry I asked you. I have made you very sad."

"I'm very tired. I'm going to bed now." My mother stands up and walks to her room. At the door, she turns around and says, "You are very much like your father." She goes into her room and shuts the door.

10. SLATE

I clean up the living room and the kitchen and go to bed. I can't sleep. I want to talk to Sei. I call him, but he doesn't answer his phone.

I send Sei a very long text. I tell him everything my mother said. It takes me a long time.

I still can't sleep, so I get up and take my cello into my bedroom. I hope my mother won't hear me playing. But it doesn't help me. No music comes out of the cello tonight and there are no new messages in my head.

Finally, I fall asleep for a few hours.

I'm making breakfast when my mother comes into the kitchen in the morning. She looks terrible. I think she has been crying all night. I think she will tell me to go to school today, but she doesn't say anything.

As soon as she leaves the apartment, I hurry to Sei's house. The gate is closed, but the door to the house isn't locked. I run up the stairs to his room. He isn't there.

I tidy and clean a little while I wait. I'm sure he will be back soon. I'm bored and worried. I go down to the kitchen to get some water. When I come back upstairs, Sei is there. His face is still black and swollen, but he is smiling. He is holding his phone. When he looks at me, I know he read my text.

But he is not alone! Sitting next to Sei is another boy. He is tall. He has spiky hair. He is wearing tight jeans and a T-shirt that says *Psychopath*.

"Wow," says the strange boy in English. "Another new person! Who are you?"

He is very relaxed. He is interested. He's not frightened. I'm pleased I studied English very hard. I worked hard at English because I thought my father was an American. I can understand him. It seems that Sei can understand him too.

"I went to the other place. Nothing happened. It seemed I was just called to look down from a high place," said Sei. "I could see the circle with the grey stones and the big stone in the middle, and I could see the circle you are making. Then I met this new friend. I don't know his name, but he talks like an American. Maybe there was a mistake, but he came back here with me. I think he is your half-brother."

"What!" The strange boy and I shout together.

"I don't believe it!" says the boy. "I don't have a sister!"

Sei laughs. "Ai, the voice said you had a half-brother in America."

I can't believe it. I ask the first question that comes into my head. "What's your name?"

"I'm Slate Forest."

"What does Slate mean?" asks Sei.

"I don't know. It's a strange name. My father gave it to me. I never asked him because he went away soon after I was born. But I know that slate is a blue-grey rock."

Sei and I look at each other.

I am so surprised, I can't talk, but Sei says. "This is Ai. I'm sure she is your sister. Her name is Ai Hayashi. It means blue forest in Japanese. I am Sei Mori. My name can mean blue forest too. The meaning of your name is almost the same, so I think we are connected."

"How old are you?" I ask.

"I'm fifteen. Why all these questions?"

"Because Ai and I have big problems. And now you are here with us. We want to understand why," says Sei.

"Where is here?" asks Slate.

"Japan," says Sei.

"Wow! How did I get here?"

"Because you are a space and time traveller," I say.

"What?" Slate looks surprised. "A space and time traveller? Are you crazy? What do you mean?"

Sei tries again. "Do you sometimes find yourself in another place? A place where you can do something special?"

"Sure. I have dreams. In my dreams I am in a green field. I can jump so high. I'm so fast. I'm amazing! I will be the greatest basketball player ever. My uniform is blue, so I guess I will play for the USA in the Olympics. But my dream is different today. I was having my basketball dream, and now I am in Japan with two people I don't know."

Sei and I look at each other. "How can we tell him?" I ask.

"I don't know, says Sei.

I have an idea. "Slate," I say. "Tell us about your father."

"I don't know a lot," says Slate. "He was in a rock band. My mother was the singer for the band. When I was born, he went away. I don't think he wanted to be a father."

"What about your mother?"

"I don't know about much about her. She died when I was eight. Do you have any Coke? I'm thirsty."

Sei gets up and brings cans of Coke from the refrigerator.

I ask, "Where do you live? Who looks after you?"

Slate drinks his Coke and says, "I don't live with anyone. I look after myself."

"But you are only fifteen! You must go to school!" I'm shouting. I have never met anyone like Slate, and I can't believe he is my father's son.

Slate gives me a bad look. "If I had a mother, I think she would talk like you!"

Sei looks at me. His look means stop shouting!

"Tell us Slate," he says quietly. "Tell us about your life."

"My mother died. So the social people came. They took me to live with a family. I think they were good people, but I didn't like them, and they didn't like me. I ran away. The social people found me, and took me to another family. They were not so nice, but maybe I was difficult. So when I was thirteen, I ran away again. That time the social people couldn't find me.

"I live on the streets. It's a good life. I have my father's guitar. I play and sing outside the railway station, and on street corners. People give me money. I have enough money for food and clothes.

"There are many young people who live on the streets in my city. They are my friends. We play basketball in the park. I am the best…"

Suddenly I hear a voice. I look at Sei and Slate. I look at their faces. They can hear the voice too.

11. THE FIRST WAR

--- 'I am the leader of the people who live on the planet Kyanyx. I will tell you our story because it is your story too.

Our people came from a world far, far away. Long ago, some of us took a spaceship and left our home to explore the universe. We travelled for hundreds of years in Earth time. It was very interesting and we learned many things. But finally we were tired. We wanted fresh air and wind and sunshine. We looked for a place where we could stop and live for a while.

We found a new home. It is a very small planet. It is a place like Earth, but it is very small. It is a place of high mountains and forests. We called it Kyanyx. In the language of our old home, it means blue forest.

People in your world sometimes call Earth the Blue Planet, but they do not know that there is another planet called Kyanyx. It is also a Blue Planet.

We thought Kyanyx was a perfect place for us to live. There were no people living there, but there were birds. Some were very big gentle birds. We called them Labdabi. They like to ride the wind and enjoy the sun. They never come to the ground.

But there were other birds. They were also very big, but they were like dragons. They liked to kill. They liked darkness and storms. We called them Mugu. The Labdabi and the Mugu were at war.

We wanted to stay there, but we could not stay if there was a war. We watched the birds and understood their ways. We found a way to communicate with the Labdabi. They told us there was a way to destroy the Mugu, the dragon birds.

Only the Great Mother of the Mugu can lay eggs. From every egg from the Great Mother come one hundred or more baby dragon birds.

The Labdabi lay many eggs and each egg produces one baby bird.

The Labdabi eggs have great power, but one of their eggs alone cannot destroy a great Mugu egg.

We learnt that we must collect Labdabi eggs and put them in a circle. Then we must steal an egg from the Great Mother of the Mugu and put it in the centre of the circle. The power from the circle of Labdabi eggs would be enough to destroy the Mugu egg. Then all the adult dragon birds, and even the Great Mother would die.

The Labdabi birds were willing to give us ten of their eggs, but we had to steal the Mugu egg.

In those days we were young and strong. It was very difficult and very dangerous, but finally we took an egg from the nest of the Great Mother. We put that egg in the middle of the circle and destroyed the egg, the Great Mother and all the dragon birds.

You have seen this circle. It is the circle of grey stones.'---

12. THE SECOND WAR

----'*For a very long time we lived in peace and happiness. We grew food. We made music. The Labdabi were our friends. It was a perfect life.*

Then there was a night of shooting stars. We were happy because the stars were so beautiful. We thought we were lucky to live in such a magical place.

But one of the shooting stars came to ground in the mountains. It gave energy to an egg from the Great Mother of the Mugu, hidden high in the mountains. The egg hatched, and in a short time there were more than a hundred dragon birds attacking and killing us.

The Labdabi hid in faraway places. They could not help us.

Many of our people died. Our blood became weak. Many children died at birth. Most of the children that survived did not live very long. We tried to fight back, but after long years of war, we had little strength or energy to fight. We knew we must do something to save our people.

We have always been space and time travellers so we know a lot about Earth. We have different powers, but we also know that Earth people are like us.

We made a plan. We sent our best and strongest warriors to Earth. We told them to find partners and have children. We thought that we should have children in many different countries. These children would grow up and make an army. We would bring the army to Kyanyx. They would fight the Mugu, and win.

At first, we thought our plan was working well. Our warriors found partners on Earth. They married Earth people. Many children were born. But there were problems. Very few of the children had our powers. And there were diseases on Earth that we do not have on Kyanyx. Even our strongest warriors got sick and died.

We could not make an army. Only four of our children on earth have our powers.

You three - Sei, Ai and Slate can come when we call you. Azurine is the youngest of our children on Earth. She is only ten in Earth years. She will be strong when she is older, but we cannot call her now.

So we only have three strong young people to come to help us. Three people cannot make an army. We thought our plan had failed. We believed it was the end of our people.

But when everything was dark, hope came to us. A brave young Labdabi saw a giant egg high in the mountains. He told the older Labdabi, and they sent a message to us.

We remembered the old stories of our people. We remembered that long ago, we defeated the Mugu by destroying a great egg of the Mother. We made a new plan.

We trained Sei and Slate to be warriors. We did not have to train Ai. Her father gave her the power to fly, and that was enough.

The Labdabi came out of hiding to help us. We asked them to give us eggs. Then we called you, Ai, to come and collect them. The Labdabi dropped their eggs into your hands, and you took them back to Earth.

Now you are taking the eggs back to the Kyanyx. There are only two more eggs to make the circle.

You must do this soon.

Then will come the most difficult task.

Ai, you must fly up to the high mountains and bring the Mugu egg down to the circle.

The Labdabi will go with you, to protect you in the air. Sei and Slate will try to distract the Mugu while you take the egg.

Then they must protect you when you fly near the ground. The Labdabi cannot go there.

When the great egg of the Mother is in the centre of the circle, the end will come. The Mugu will be destroyed and the people of Kyanyx will be safe.'---

13. AI SAYS GOODBYE TO HER MOTHER

"Who was that guy? What kind of fairy tale is this?" asks Slate. "I never heard anything so crazy!"

"It's not crazy," says Sei. "Look at my face! I was attacked by one of the dragon birds."

Slate shakes his head. "I'm going to wake up on my street corner. There will be money from kind people on the ground. I will take the money and my guitar, and go to my favourite hamburger restaurant."

I jump up. "I have to go home!" I say.

I run out of Sei's house and go back to the apartment. I know the story now. Everything is happening too quickly. I know I must take the last eggs to the circle.

I hurry to the balcony outside my mother's room. I sit in the chair, and almost at once I'm flying with the last two eggs to the circle.

It's very strange. Everything is very quiet, but high above me I think I can hear the sound of wings. Are they the Labdabi or the Mugu? I don't know.

I fly down to the stone circle in the green field. I put the last two eggs in their places. The circle is finished!

Usually, I'm back in the chair on the balcony as soon as my delivery is finished. But this time is different. I rise higher and higher. I'm above the mountains, but I'm not frightened. I feel like I'm lying on a soft bed. All around me I hear quiet sounds. After a while, the sounds become words. "You have done well. Now, look at the old nest of the Mother of the Mugu. This is where you must come to take the egg."

I look down and I feel sick. There is a pain in my head. Far below me is a black, rocky mountain. A very big black bird is sitting on top of the mountain. Or is it a dragon?

I'm back in the chair on the balcony. I look at my phone. 5:30! My mother will not come home for four hours. Then I hear a key in the door and my mother's voice.

"Ai! Ai! Where are you? I came home early because I was worried about you."

I feel very tired, but I get up from the chair and walk into my mother's bedroom.

I walk over to my mother and hug her. "I love you," I say.

She looks at me. She sees something in my face. "You're going away," she says in a very quiet voice. "I'm going to lose you too."

I feel terrible. "I don't want to go, but I have to," I say. "I will try to come back. I want to come back. I'm not like my father."

My mother turns away from me. She goes to the closet in her room and takes a box from a high shelf. She opens it.

She takes out a photograph. "This is your father and me on our wedding day."

I'm crying. I'm crying so hard I can't see the photograph.

Then she takes my hand and puts a ring on my finger. "The day we got married, your father took this ring from his finger and put it on my finger. Maybe it will bring you luck. Maybe it will bring you back to me."

"I love you. I will come back," I say. Then I run out of the apartment and down the stairs. I don't stop running until I get to Sei's house. I cry all the way.

Sei and Slate are waiting for me. Slate looks serious.

"Do you understand now?" I ask him.

"Maybe. I don't know," he says. "Sei told me everything. I can't believe it. I don't want to believe it. He says we are going to fight, and maybe we will die. And he says I can't stop it."

Sei asks me, "Are you OK?"

"No! I said goodbye to my mother!"

Sei pours water onto a towel and gives it to me. I wash my eyes and I feel a little better. I sit down at the table with Sei and Slate. Sei holds my hand. His hand is cold. I look at him. He looks older and stronger.

"Slate," says Sei. "Hold your sister's hand."

Slate takes my hand. His hand is warm. He smiles at me. "I have a sister," he says, but he has no time to say more.

14. THE BATTLE

I'm in the air. I can see the green field with the old circle of grey stones, and the new circle of blue and black stones.

I can see Sei and Slate. Sei has a sword. He is shouting. His sword is pointing up to the sky. There is light coming from the sword. It's very bright. It's like a laser. It hurts my eyes.

Suddenly, the blue sky and sunlight are gone. Everything is dark, and there is a terrible noise. The sky is full of very big black birds, or maybe they are dragons.

I don't know what to do. I can't see Sei or Slate. The dragon birds are diving down towards the green field. Then they stop. They are floating in the air. I think they are waiting for something.

The noise is louder. I'm up in the sky. I have no control. The giant dragon bird I saw on the mountain is flying past me.

I hear Sei's voice in my head. "Now, Ai. Now! Get the egg!"

I don't know if I can fly higher. But I know I must try. I can't do it! I have no energy! I'm falling!

Then I think, *I can't die now. I told my mother I would come back.* The thought gives me a little more power, and I rise up towards the high mountain.

Then the soft pillows and the quiet sounds are around me. I feel safe. The Labdabi have come to protect me. Up and up I fly. I am looking at the place where the giant dragon bird was sitting. But the bird is not there. I can see the Mugu egg. I fly towards it.

"We cannot come closer", say the voices of the Labdabi. "You must do this alone."

I can't! I can't! I think. But then I think, *Sei and Slate are on the ground. They are fighting the giant dragon birds. I must do this.*

I pick up the egg. It is so heavy, and it feels evil. My body is so painful. I think my head will explode, but I fly towards the ground and again the warm, soft, kind Labdabi are all around me.

They go with me towards the green field. They are with me when I pass the circle of dragon birds. Then they are gone.

I look down. The giant dragon bird is attacking Sei and Slate. Sei fires light beams from his sword. The giant bird flies towards Slate, but Slate jumps so high and runs so fast. The enemy cannot catch him.

Sei sees me and shouts, "Now Slate!" I'm flying to the centre of the circle when I see Slate run towards the giant bird. No, Slate! Run away!

But Slate jumps very high in the air and catches the bird's tail. He jumps again and is on the bird's back. Sei is sending light beams to the bird's eyes.

The bird turns left and right. I know I must take the stone to the ground now. I dive down. I am closer and closer to the centre of the circle!

I am near the ground when Slate falls past me. I look up and see the dragon bird. It is so close to me, I can see its red eyes and feel the heat from its fiery breath. Oh no! It's going to kill me. We have failed!

I drop the egg and put my hands in front of my face. Then a great red flame comes out of the ring on my finger. It hits the dragon bird, and the bird goes backwards.

Everything happens very quickly. The egg falls to the centre of the circle.

It's so strange. There was noise and light and flames, but suddenly it is very quiet.

The eggs in the outer circle are flashing. The dragon egg I dropped in the middle of the circle turns red and then black.

I'm still in the air when all the stones become grey.

I see Slate lying on the ground. So I come down to the ground and run to him. "Are you OK?" I shout.

Slate rolls over and smiles. "Did you see me jump? I'm amazing."

Sei walks towards us. "We did it," he says. "The Mugu are gone and Kyanyx is safe. Now we must go to the castle." He points to the big stone building at the end of the green field.

Slate and I follow Sei to the castle. The door is open. When we walk into the front hall, we see many people. They are old. They have white hair. They are very happy. They are shouting and smiling.

"Welcome!" they shout. "You have saved our planet. You have saved us!"

Sei says, "Where is your leader? Where is the man who brought us here?"

The people become quiet. A very small, very old man says, "Come with me."

He walks to the back of the castle. Sei, Slate and I follow him. All the people from the front hall walk behind us.

There is a man lying on a bed in a very luxurious and beautiful room.

His white hair is very long, and his beard goes down to his waist. His eyes are closed, but when Sei asks, "Who are you?" he opens his eyes.

But he doesn't answer Sei's question. He says, "Welcome my grandson. I am dying. You are the leader of our people now."

He closes his eyes, and the people who followed us into the room start crying and shouting. Then they turn to Sei and say, "You are our new leader!"

15. AI GOES HOME

I ask about the ring my mother gave me. The ring that saved us all. The very small, very old man tells me.

"It's a love ring. It has great power. We saw it on your finger. When you were in danger, our old leader put all his love for his grandson into the ring. It killed him. But I don't think his love was enough. I think your father loved your mother very much. Your mother loves you. You love your mother. That love gave the ring extra power. Enough power to beat the giant Mugu bird."

Sei stays on Kyanyx. He is the new leader. He wants me to stay, but I want to go back to Earth. I promised my mother.

I go back to the apartment. I say to my mother, "I said I would come back." I tell her everything.

Sei gives me his house. My mother and I move to Sei's house. My mother does not have to pay rent on the apartment. There is more money. Life is easier.

My mother tells my school some crazy story. It's OK. I can go back to school. Life is normal, but now I go home to Sei's house. I play my cello, but I don't fly.

Sometimes Sei comes to visit me. He always says, "Please come back to Kyanyx."

I say, "Maybe one day."

My mother and I go to France for a vacation. We find Azurine. She is a student at a very famous music school. We go to hear her play in a concert. She is very good. I don't want to meet her because I hope her life will be normal. I hope she never has to help the people on Kyanyx.

And Slate? My crazy half-brother? Slate wanted to go back to the USA. He said life on Kyanyx was too boring.

I don't know how Sei arranged everything, but Slate lives with a family he likes very much. He has a basketball scholarship at a high school. If he does well, he will get a scholarship to university. Maybe one day he will play basketball for the USA.

THANK YOU

Thank you for reading Children of Another Planet (Word count: 10,802) We hope you enjoyed it.

If you would like to read more graded readers, please visit our website http://www.italkyoutalk.com

Other Level 3 graded readers include
A Dangerous Weekend
A Holiday to Remember
Akiko and Amy Part 1
Akiko and Amy Part 2
Akiko and Amy Part 3
Be My Valentine
Different Seas
Enjoy Your Business Trip
Enjoy Your Homestay
I'm Late!
I Need a Friend
Let's Do It!
Lincoln Takes a Trip
Match Day
Old Jack's Ghost Stories from England (1)
Old Jack's Ghost Stories from England (2)
Old Jack's Ghost Stories from Ireland
Old Jack's Ghost Stories from Japan

Old Jack's Ghost Stories from Scotland
Old Jack's Ghost Stories from Wales
Party Time!
Pretty and Bright
Roger's Long Ride
Rona
Stories for Christmas
Summer Days
The Curse
The Diary
Time to Go
Together Again
Travellers' Tales
Wall of Secrets
Who is Holly?
Wintertime

ABOUT THE AUTHOR

I Talk You Talk Press is an award-winning Japan-based publisher of language textbooks, graded readers and language learning/teaching resources. We won the Language Learner Literature Award in 2019 and 2020.

Our team is made up of highly experienced language teachers and translators, who have all studied at least one additional language to an advanced level.

This experience enables us to design our materials from the perspective of both the teacher and the learner. We consult with both teachers and language learners when designing our textbooks and graded readers, and test our materials extensively in the classroom before publication.

We are a fast-growing press, and currently publish graded readers for learners of English. We publish new graded readers monthly.